To

....

From

....

Date

....

Serenity

Promises of Hope and Peace

summerside
PRESS

Summerside Press™
Minneapolis, MN 55337
www.summersidepress.com

Serenity

© 2011 by Summerside Press

ISBN 978-1-60936-245-4

Unless otherwise noted, Scripture quotations are taken from The Holy
Bible, New International Version®, NIV®. Copyright © 1973, 1978, 1984,
2011 by Biblica, Inc.™ Used by permission of Zondervan. All rights reserved
worldwide. Other Scripture references are from the following sources:
The New American Standard Bible® (NASB). Copyright © 1960, 1962, 1963,
1968, 1971, 1972, 1973, 1975, 1977, 1995 by The Lockman Foundation. Used
by permission. The New King James Version (NKJV). Copyright © 1982 by
Thomas Nelson, Inc. Used by permission. The Holy Bible, New Living
Translation (NLT), copyright © 1996, 2004. Used by permission of Tyndale
House Publishers, Inc., Wheaton, Illinois. *The Message* (MSG). Copyright
© 1993, 1994, 1995, 1996, 2000, 2001, 2002 by Eugene Peterson. Used by
permission of NavPress, Colorado Springs, CO. The New Century
Version® (NCV). Copyright © 1987, 1988, 1991 by Thomas Nelson, Inc.
Used by permission. All rights reserved.

Stock or custom editions of Summerside Press titles may be purchased in
bulk for educational, business, ministry, fundraising, or sales promotional
use. For information, please e-mail specialmarkets@summersidepress.com.

Compiled by Jill Olson
Designed by Lisa and Jeff Franke

*Summerside Press™ is an inspirational publisher offering fresh, irresistible books
to uplift the heart and engage the mind.*

Printed in the USA.

Contents

God grant me the serenity
to accept the things I cannot change;
courage to change the things I can;
and wisdom to know the difference.

Living one day at a time;
enjoying one moment at a time;
accepting hardships as the pathway to peace;
taking, as He did, this sinful world
as it is, not as I would have it;
Trusting that He will make all things right
if I surrender to His Will;
that I may be reasonably happy in this life
and supremely happy with Him
forever in the next. Amen.

REINHOLD NIEBUHR

Introduction

We all long for peace and serenity, for change.
Sometimes desperately. But often we don't have
the wisdom to know what we can change and what
we can't. And the courage to change the things we
can may be outside our grasp. Thankfully, God gives
both wisdom and strength to those who reach
toward His open arms.

Serenity is a collection of life-changing verses and
motivating quotes selected to encourage anyone
seeking God's peace. The twelve chapters reflect the
Scripture-based 12-step program used in recovery
groups worldwide. They guide readers to journey one
step at a time, hand in hand with God, toward
the abundant life He has promised. One filled with
lasting wholeness, purpose, and joy.

"For I know the plans I have for you," declares the LORD,
"plans to prosper you...to give you hope and a future."
JEREMIAH 29:11

ONE

Acceptance

*God grant me the serenity
to accept the things I cannot change;
courage to change the things I can;
and wisdom to know the difference.*

For by grace you have been saved through faith;
and that not of yourselves.

EPHESIANS 2:8 NASB

[God] is looking for people who will come in simple
dependence upon His grace, and rest in simple
faith upon His greatness. At this very moment,
He's looking at you.

JACK HAYFORD

The LORD is the everlasting God,
the Creator of all the earth.
He never grows weak or weary....
He gives power to the weak
and strength to the powerless.

ISAIAH 40:28-29 NLT

God often calls us to do things that we do not have
the ability to do.... If God calls you to do something,
God empowers you to do it.

SUZANNE FARNHAM

Because we are spiritual beings...it is for our good,
individually and collectively, to live our lives in
interactive dependence upon God.

DALLAS WILLARD

We know and rely on the love God has for us.

1 JOHN 4:16

We may...depend upon God's promises,
for...He will be as good as His word.
He is so kind that He cannot deceive us,
so true that He cannot break His promise.

MATTHEW HENRY

The Lord your God fights for you,
just as he has promised.

JOSHUA 23:10 NLT

Love means
to love that which is unlovable,
or it is no virtue at all;
forgiving means to pardon
that which is unpardonable,
or it is no virtue at all—
and to hope means hoping
when things are hopeless,
or it is no virtue at all.

G. K. CHESTERTON

How calmly may we commit ourselves
to the hands of Him who bears up the world.

JOHN PAUL RICHTER

He [God] knows everything about us.
And He cares about everything. Moreover, He can
manage every situation. And He loves us!

HANNAH WHITALL SMITH

The revelation of GOD is whole
and pulls our lives together.
The signposts of GOD are clear
and point out the right road.
The life-maps of GOD are right,
showing the way to joy.

PSALM 19:7–8 MSG

The more we depend on God
the more dependable we find He is.

CLIFF RICHARD

The God who made the whole world
and everything in it is the Lord of the land
and the sky. He does not live in temples built by
human hands. This God is the One who gives life,
breath, and everything else to people.

ACTS 17:24–25 NCV

I don't think there is anyone who needs God's help
and grace as much as I do. Sometimes I feel so
helpless and weak. I think that is why God uses me.
Because I cannot depend on my own strength, I rely
on Him twenty-four hours a day.

MOTHER TERESA

Yet this I call to mind and therefore I have hope:
Because of the LORD's great love
we are not consumed,
for his compassions never fail.
They are new every morning;
great is your faithfulness.

LAMENTATIONS 3:21-23

When we realize He's bigger than anything
we can get our minds around,
we can begin to relax and enjoy Him.

PAULA RHINEHART

He makes wars cease to the end of the earth....
Be still, and know that I am God

PSALM 46:9-10 NKJV

My power is made perfect in weakness.

2 CORINTHIANS 12:9

God does not allow us to continue
to reduce Him to a size and a shape
we can manage. He moves in our lives
in ways that burst our categories
and overwhelm our finiteness.

Ah Lord GOD! Behold, You have made
the heavens and the earth by Your great power
and by Your outstretched arm!
Nothing is too difficult for You.

JEREMIAH 32:17 NASB

What matters supremely is not the fact that
I know God, but the larger fact which
underlies it—the fact that He knows me.
I am graven on the palms of His hands. I am never
out of His mind. All my knowledge of Him
depends on His sustained initiative in knowing me.
I know Him because He first knew me,
and continues to know me.

J. I. PACKER

Success does not depend on a commitment
to effort or perfection, but to trust.

NEVA COYLE

O Sovereign LORD.... Is there any god
in heaven or on earth who can perform
such great and mighty deeds as you do?

DEUTERONOMY 3:24 NLT

The goal of much that is written about in life
management is to enable us to do more in less time.
But is this necessarily a desirable goal? Perhaps we
need to get less done, but the right things.

JEAN FLEMMING

I will cry to God Most High,
To God who accomplishes all things for me.

PSALM 57:2 NASB

[God] stands fast as your rock,
steadfast as your safeguard, sleepless as your watcher,
valiant as your champion.

CHARLES H. SPURGEON

Simplicity means a return to the posture of
dependence. Like children we live in a spirit of trust.
What we have we receive as a gift.

RICHARD J. FOSTER

Because God is responsible for our welfare, we are
told to cast all our care upon Him, for He cares for
us. God says, "I'll take the burden—don't give it a
thought—leave it to Me." God is keenly aware that we
are dependent upon Him for life's necessities.

BILLY GRAHAM

How you have helped the powerless!
How you have saved the arm that is feeble!

JOB 26:2

God Incarnate is the end of fear;
and the heart that realizes that He is in the midst,
that takes heed to the assurance of His loving
presence, will be quiet in the midst of alarm.

F. B. MEYER

Your love, LORD, reaches to the heavens,
your faithfulness to the skies.

PSALM 36:5

"Blessed are the poor in spirit."
Not poor in substance, but spirit.
This first beatitude has nothing to do with being
materially destitute or financially bankrupt.
Jesus is placing value on a humble spirit,
on those who acknowledge a spiritual bankruptcy
in and of themselves. Where there is an absence of
well-polished pride and personal conceit, there is a
wholesome dependence on the living God.

CHARLES R. SWINDOLL

I know, O LORD, that a man's way is not in himself,
Nor is it in a man who walks to direct his steps.

JEREMIAH 10:23 NASB

There's a quiet, serene confidence
in knowing that all things do not stand or fall
according to one's own achievements or the
correctness of every decision one makes.

JOSEPH A. SITTLER

Your love is comfort in sadness,
quietness in tumult, rest in weariness,
hope in despair.

MARION C. GARRETTY

You can't change circumstances and you can't change
other people, but God can change you.

EVELYN A. THEISSEN

You, O Lord, are a God of compassion and mercy,
slow to get angry and filled with unfailing love
and faithfulness. Look down and have mercy on me.
Give your strength to your servant.

PSALM 86:15–16 NLT

I abide in Christ and in doing so I find rest,
and the peace of God which passes
all understanding fills my heart and life.

JOHN HUNTER

God is our refuge and strength,
an ever-present help in trouble.

PSALM 46:1

Do not withhold your mercy from me, LORD;
may your love and faithfulness always protect me.

PSALM 40:11

I am a mighty God. Nothing is too difficult for Me....
Your weakness is designed to open you up
to My Power. Therefore, do not fear your
limitations or measure the day's demands
against your strength. What I require of you
is to stay connected to Me, living in trusting
dependence on My limitless resources.
When you face unexpected demands,
there is no need to panic. Remember that I am
with you. Talk with Me, and listen while I talk you
through each challenging situation.

SARAH YOUNG

Trust God from the bottom of your heart;
don't try to figure out everything on your own.
Listen for God's voice in everything you do,
everywhere you go;
he's the one who will keep you on track.

PROVERBS 3:5-7 MSG

You are God's created beauty and the focus
of His affection and delight.

JANET L. SMITH

It is only when Christ dwells within our hearts,
radiating the pure light of His love through our
humanity, that we discover who we are
and what we were intended to be.
There is no other joy...that is more complete.

WENDY MOORE

Jesus said to him, "I am the way,
the truth, and the life."

JOHN 14:6 NKJV

The God who created, names,
and numbers the stars in the heavens
also numbers the hairs of my head....
He pays attention to very big things
and to very small ones. What matters to me
matters to Him, and that changes my life.

ELISABETH ELLIOT

A hostile world! I call to GOD,
I cry to God to help me.
From His palace He hears my call;
my cry brings me right into His presence—
a private audience!

PSALM 18:6 MSG

Over the margins of life comes a whisper,
a faint call, a premonition of richer living
which we know we are passing by.
Strained by the very mad pace
of our daily outer burdens...we have hints
that there is a way of life vastly richer
and deeper...a life of unhurried serenity
and peace and power.

THOMAS R. KELLY

Two [kinds of people] please God —
the one who serves Him with all his heart
because he knows Him, and the one who seeks Him
with all his heart because he knows Him not.

PANNIN

Call to Me and I will answer you, and I will tell you
great and mighty things, which you do not know.

JEREMIAH 33:3 NASB

Comfort and prosperity have never enriched
the world as adversity has done....
Out of suffering and tears have come
the greatest spirits and the most blessed lives.

BILLY GRAHAM

To live by grace means to acknowledge
my whole life story, the light side and the dark.
In admitting my shadow side I learn who I am
and what God's grace means.

BRENNAN MANNING

The LORD is like a father to his children,
tender and compassionate to those who fear him.
For he knows how weak we are;
he remembers we are only dust.

PSALM 103:13-14 NLT

All those who live with any degree of serenity
live by some assurance of grace.

REINHOLD NIEBUHR

Commit your way to the LORD,
Trust also in Him, and He shall bring it to pass.

PSALM 37:5 NKJV

We come closest to God at our lowest moments.

TERRY ANDERSON

TWO

Greater Is He

*God grant me the serenity
to accept the things I cannot change;
courage to change the things I can;
and wisdom to know the difference.*

Greater is He who is in you
than he who is in the world.

1 JOHN 4:4 NASB

Trust is giving up what little I have
in strength and power so I can confidently relax
in His power and strength.

GLORIA GAITHER

God is here, right here, on his way
to put things right and redress all wrongs.
He's on his way! He'll save you!"

ISAIAH 35:3 MSG

I will restore to you the years that the swarming
locust has eaten.... You shall eat in plenty
and be satisfied, and praise the name of the LORD.

JOEL 2:25-26 NKJV

Live near to God, and so all things will appear to you
little in comparison with eternal realities.

ROBERT MURRAY MCCHEYNE

It is through man's encounter with God
that he reaches his highest destiny.

CAROL GISH

The center of God's will is our only safety.

BETSIE TEN BOOM

No king is saved by the size of his army;
no warrior escapes by his great strength.
A horse is a vain hope for deliverance;
despite all its great strength it cannot save.
But the eyes of the LORD are on those who fear him,
on those whose hope is in his unfailing love

PSALM 33:16-18

I will both lie down in peace, and sleep;
For You alone, O LORD, make me dwell in safety.

PSALM 4:8 NKJV

Only God can keep all His promises.

JANETTE OKE

Praise the LORD who has given rest to his people…
just as he promised. Not one word has failed
of all the wonderful promises he gave.

1 KINGS 8:56 NLT

The Gospel does not consist of what we can do for ourselves, but of what God stands ready to do for us.

See, I am doing a new thing! Now it springs up;
do you not perceive it?
I am making a way in the wilderness
and streams in the wasteland.

ISAIAH 43:19

It is God's will for you to have your dignity and security restored. You don't need to wrestle with this one.... In fact, if you're willing to exercise the kind of boldness that excites the heart of God, you can go right ahead and thank Him in advance because you know that what you've asked is as good as done. Sometimes we see or sense the evidence immediately. Other times God lets it amass bit by bit.

BETH MOORE

Faithful is He who calls you,
and He also will bring it to pass.

1 THESSALONIANS 5:24 NASB

You don't have to see the whole flight
of stairs at once, just the first step.
After you've taken that one,
then you will see the next one.
It's just one step at a time.

It won't be long before this generous God
who has great plans for us in Christ—
eternal and glorious plans they are!—
will have you put together and on your feet for good.
He gets the last word.

1 PETER 5:10–11 MSG

The great Easter truth is not that we are to live
newly after death, but that we are to be new here
and now by the power of the Resurrection.

PHILLIPS BROOKS

The dark threads are as needful
in the Weaver's skillful hand
As the threads of gold and silver
in the pattern He has planned.

We now have this light shining in our hearts,
but we ourselves are like fragile clay jars
containing this great treasure. This makes
it clear that our great power is from God,
not from ourselves.

2 CORINTHIANS 4:7 NLT

What God does in time, He planned from eternity.
And all that He planned in eternity
He carries out in time....
No part of His eternal plan changes.

J. I. PACKER

For this is what the high and exalted One says—
he who lives forever, whose name is holy: "I live in
a high and holy place, but also with the one who is
contrite and lowly in spirit, to revive the spirit
of the lowly and to revive the heart of the contrite."

ISAIAH 57:15

Prayer is the way to open ourselves to God,
and the way in which He shows us our unstable hearts
and begins to strengthen them.

TERESA OF AVILA

No pain, no palm; no thorns, no throne;
no gall, no glory; no cross, no crown.

WILLIAM PENN

Heal me, O LORD, and I will be healed; save me and I
will be saved, for You are my praise.

JEREMIAH 17:14 NASB

Only Christ himself, who slept in the boat in the
storm and then spoke calm to the wind and waves,
can stand beside us when we are in a panic and say to
us: Peace. It will not be explainable.... And there is
nothing else like it in the whole wide world.

ELISABETH ELLIOT

God gives His gifts where He finds the vessel
empty enough to receive them.

C. S. LEWIS

I pray that from his glorious, unlimited resources he
will empower you with inner strength through his
Spirit. Then Christ will make his home in your hearts
as you trust in him. Your roots will grow down into
God's love and keep you strong.

EPHESIANS 3:16–17 NLT

This is what I found out about religion:
it gives you courage to make the decisions
you must make in a crisis, and then the confidence
to leave the result to a higher power.

DWIGHT D. EISENHOWER

One thing Jesus asks of me: that I lean upon Him;
that in Him alone I put complete trust;
that I surrender myself to Him unreservedly.

MOTHER TERESA

I am the vine; you are the branches.
If you remain in me and I in you, you will bear
much fruit; apart from me you can do nothing.

JOHN 15:5

To accept the responsibility of being
a child of God is to accept
every good thing that life offers you.

STELLA MANN

Life is meant to be lived from a Center, a divine
Center...a Life who speaks in us and through us to the
world. We have all heard this holy Whisper at times....
But too many of us have heeded the Voice only at
times.... We have not counted this Holy Thing within
us to be the most precious thing in the world.

THOMAS R. KELLY

I am the light of the world. The person
who follows me will never live in darkness
but will have the light that gives life.

JOHN 8:12 NCV

God is every moment totally aware of each one of us.
Totally aware in intense concentration and love.

EUGENIA PRICE

I rejoice in your promise
like one who finds great spoil.

PSALM 119:162

In other religions, one must be purified
before he can knock at the door;
in Christianity, one knocks on the door as a sinner,
and He who answers us heals.

FULTON J. SHEEN

I stand at the door and knock.
If anyone hears my voice and opens the door,
I will come in.

REVELATION 3:20

He was wounded for our transgressions,
He was bruised for our iniquities;
The chastisement for our peace was upon Him,
And by His stripes we are healed.

ISAIAH 53:5 NKJV

Any man who does not believe
in miracles is not a realist.

DAVID BEN-GURION

Hope is not a granted wish or a favor performed;
no, it is far greater than that. It is a zany,
unpredictable dependence on a God
who loves to surprise us out of our socks.

MAX LUCADO

If God gives such attention to the appearance of
wildflowers...don't you think he'll attend to you...?
What I'm trying to do here is to get you to relax,
to not be so preoccupied with *getting*,
so you can respond to God's *giving*.

MATTHEW 6:30-31 MSG

You are great and do marvelous deeds;
you alone are God.

PSALM 86:10

All [God's] glory and beauty come from within,
and there He delights to dwell. His visits there are
frequent, His conversation sweet, His comforts
refreshing, His peace passing all understanding.

THOMAS À KEMPIS

Instead of worrying, pray. Let petitions and praises
shape your worries into prayers, letting God know
your concerns. Before you know it, a sense of God's
wholeness, everything coming together for good,
will come and settle you down.

PHILIPPIANS 4:6–7 MSG

The secret of the mystery is: God is always greater.
No matter how great we think Him to be,
His love is always greater.

BRENNAN MANNING

I pray that the eyes of your heart may
be enlightened in order that you may know
the hope to which He has called you.

EPHESIANS 1:18

The statutes of the LORD are right,
rejoicing the heart;
The command of the LORD is pure,
enlightening the eyes.

PSALM 19:8 NKJV

May God give you more and more mercy,
peace, and love.

JUDE 1:2 NLT

Blessed is the one who trusts in the LORD,
whose confidence is in him.
They will be like a tree planted by the water
that sends out its roots by the stream.
It does not fear when heat comes;
its leaves are always green.
It has no worries in a year of drought
and never fails to bear fruit.

JEREMIAH 17:7–8

God came to us because God wanted to
join us on the road, to listen to our story,
and to help us realize that we are not
walking in circles but moving toward
the house of peace and joy.

HENRI J. M. NOUWEN

Every good and perfect gift is from above,
coming down from the Father
of the heavenly lights, who does not change
like shifting shadows.

JAMES 1:17

Life from the Center is a life of unhurried peace,
and power. It is simple. It is serene....
We need not get frantic. He is at the helm.
And when our little day is done we lie down
quietly in peace, for all is well.

THOMAS R. KELLY

Steep yourself in God-reality, God-initiative,
God-provisions. You'll find all your
everyday human concerns will be met.

LUKE 12:30–31 MSG

When we trust, the Lord works.
What is done is not done by us, but by Him.

HANNAH WHITALL SMITH

THREE

In His Hands

God grant me the serenity
to accept the things I cannot change;
courage to change the things I can;
and wisdom to know the difference.

I entrust my spirit into your hand.
Rescue me, LORD, for you are a faithful God.

PSALM 31:5 NLT

He who dwells in the secret place
of the Most High shall abide under the shadow
of the Almighty. I will say of the LORD,
"He is my refuge and my fortress; my God,
in Him I will trust."

PSALM 91:1–2 NKJV

Do not take over much thought for tomorrow.
God, who has led you safely on so far,
will lead you on to the end.
Be altogether at rest in the loving
holy confidence which you ought to have
in His heavenly Providence.

FRANCIS DE SALES

It is not objective proof of God's
existence that we want but the experience
of God's presence. That is the miracle
we are really after, and that is also,
I think, the miracle that we really get.

FREDERICK BUECHNER

You keep track of all my sorrows.
You have collected all my tears in your bottle.
You have recorded each one in your book.

PSALM 56:8 NLT

That is God's call to us—simply to be people who are
content to live close to Him and to renew the kind
of life in which the closeness is felt and experienced.

THOMAS MERTON

The LORD is your keeper;
The LORD is your shade on your right hand....
The LORD will protect you from all evil;
He will keep your soul.
The LORD will guard your going out
and your coming in
From this time forth and forever.

PSALM 121:5, 7–8 NASB

You are a child of your heavenly Father.
Confide in Him. Your faith in His love and power
can never be bold enough.

BASILEA SCHLINK

Since...we are utterly incapable of living the glorious
lives God wills for us, God did it for us.
Out of sheer generosity he put us in right standing
with himself. A pure gift.

ROMANS 3:21 MSG

God makes a promise—faith believes it,
hope anticipates it, patience quietly awaits it.

Lord, grant me a quiet mind,
that trusting Thee,
for Thou art kind,
I may go on without a fear,
for Thou, my Lord,
art always near.

AMY CARMICHAEL

He tends his flock like a shepherd: He gathers the
lambs in his arms and carries them close to his heart.

ISAIAH 40:11

What can harm thee, when all must first touch God,
within whom thou hast enclosed thyself?

ROBERT LEIGHTON

With each new experience of letting God
be in control, we gain courage and reinforcement
for daring to do it again and again.

GLORIA GAITHER

Your success does not depend upon the brilliancy and
the impetuosity with which you take hold, but upon
the everlasting and sanctified bull-doggedness with
which you hang on after you have taken hold.

DR. A. B. MELDRUM

You will show me the path of life;
In Your presence is fullness of joy;
At Your right hand are pleasures forevermore.

PSALM 16:11 NKJV

Good friend, always be open to the miracle
of the second chance.

DAVID STIER

The Lord is faithful, and he will strengthen you
and protect you

2 THESSALONIANS 3:3

I am the good shepherd.
The good shepherd gives his life for the sheep.

JOHN 10:11 NCV

God never abandons anyone on whom
He has set His love; nor does Christ,
the good shepherd, ever lose track of His sheep.

J. I. PACKER

Trust in the LORD forever, for in GOD the LORD,
we have an everlasting Rock.

ISAIAH 26:4 NASB

In heaven our light will be provided by an infallible
source, the Son of God. And nothing will interfere
with our basking in His fellowship.

MARILYN M. MORGAN

God wishes to be seen,
and He wishes to be sought,
and He wishes to be expected,
and He wishes to be trusted.

JULIAN OF NORWICH

In darkness there is no choice.
It is light that enables us to see the differences
between things; and it is Christ who gives us light.

AUGUSTUS W. HARE

You changed my sorrow into dancing.
You took away my clothes of sadness,
and clothed me in happiness.

PSALM 30:11 NCV

O Lord, show Your mercy to me
and gladden my heart.
I am like the man on the way to Jericho
who was overtaken by robbers,
wounded, and left for dead:
O Good Samaritan,
come to my aid.
I am like the sheep that went astray:
O Good Shepherd,
seek me out and bring me home
in accord with Your will.
Let me dwell in Your house
all the days of my life
and praise You forever and ever.

JEROME

Enter into the inner chamber of your mind.
Shut out all things save God
and whatever may aid you in seeking God;
and having barred the door of your chamber,
seek Him.

ANSELM OF CANTERBURY

Be strong and let your heart take courage,
All you who hope in the LORD.

PSALM 31:24 NASB

I used to think that God's gifts were on shelves—
one above another—and the taller we grow,
the easier we can reach them. Now I find that God's
gifts are on shelves—one beneath another—
and the lower we stoop, the more we get.

F. B. MEYER

But I, by your great love,
can come into your house;
in reverence I bow down

PSALM 5:7

Let my soul take refuge...beneath the
shadow of Your wings:
let my heart, this sea of restless waves,
find peace in You, O God.

AUGUSTINE

I long to dwell in your tent forever
and take refuge in the shelter of your wings.

PSALM 61:4

I will also meditate on all Your work,
And talk of Your deeds.
Your way, O God, is in the sanctuary;
Who is so great a God as our God?
You are the God who does wonders;
You have declared Your strength among the peoples.

PSALM 77:12–14 NKJV

The raging storms may round us beat
We'll never leave our safe retreat
O Rock divine, O Refuge dear,
Be Thou our Helper ever near:
A Shelter in the time of storm.

VERNON J. CHARLESWORTH

Why should we live halfway up the hill and swathed
in the mists, when we might have an unclouded sky
and a radiant sun over our heads if we would
climb higher and walk in the light of His face?

ALEXANDER MACLAREN

"For the mountains may be removed and the hills
may shake, but my lovingkindness will not be removed
from you, and my covenant of peace will not be
shaken," says the LORD who has compassion on you.

ISAIAH 54:10 NASB

We are made for God, and nothing less
will really satisfy us.

BRENNAN MANNING

I am leaving you with a gift—peace of mind and heart.
And the peace I give is a gift the world cannot give.
So don't be troubled or afraid.

JOHN 14:27 NLT

Tell me in the morning about Your love,
because I trust you. Show me what I should do,
because my prayers go up to you.

PSALM 143:8 NCV

Imagine yourself as a living house.
God comes in to rebuild that house.... You thought
you were going to be made into a decent little
cottage: but He is building a palace.
He intends to come and live in it Himself.

C. S. LEWIS

Keep me as the apple of Your eye;
Hide me under the shadow of Your wings.

PSALM 17:8 NKJV

Dear Father...give me the peace that comes
from knowing that where I am, You are,
and together we can handle whatever comes.

PAM KIDD

Let us hold unswervingly to the hope we profess,
for he who promised is faithful.

HEBREWS 10:23

As we follow Him who is everlasting
we will touch the things that last forever.
Let your faith in Christ, the omnipresent One,
be in the quiet confidence
that He will every day and every moment
keep you as the apple of His eye,
keep you in perfect peace.

ANDREW MURRAY

We wait in hope for the LORD;
he is our help and our shield.
In him our hearts rejoice,
for we trust in his holy name.
May your unfailing love be with us, LORD,
even as we put our hope in you.

PSALM 33:20-22

FOUR

Search My Heart

God grant me the serenity
to accept the things I cannot change;
courage to change the things I can;
and wisdom to know the difference.

Search me, O God, and know my heart;
Try me and know my anxious thoughts;
And see if there be any hurtful way in me,
And lead me in the everlasting way.

PSALM 139:23-24 NASB

When you are very conscious of your faults,
do not be discouraged by them, but confess them
to God. Do not excuse them, or accuse Him.
Then, peaceably resume your usual practice
of love and adoration of God.

BROTHER LAWRENCE

God is...ready to help when we need him.
We stand fearless at the cliff-edge of doom,
courageous in seastorm and earthquake,
Before the rush and roar of oceans,
the tremors that shift mountains.

PSALM 46:1-3 MSG

Beloved, whatever we are gripping to bring
us the satisfaction is a lie—unless it is Christ.
He is the Truth that sets us free

BETH MOORE

[God] does not give Himself to us fully
until we fully give ourselves to Him.

TERESA OF AVILA

God did not tell us to follow Him because
He needed our help, but because
He knew that loving Him would make us whole.

IRENAEUS

Confessing sin does more than just "patch up"
our lives; it gives us a brand new start.

JANETTE OKE

Courage is fear that has said its prayers.

DOROTHY BERNARD

I will give them a heart to know Me,
for I am the LORD;
and they will be My people,
and I will be their God,
for they will return to Me with their whole heart.

JEREMIAH 24:7 NASB

God, with all His giving heart,
can only give us Himself as we recognize
the depth of the need in our own lives.

EUGENIA PRICE

God doesn't remember my mistakes.
For all the things He does do,
this is one thing He refuses to do.
He refuses to keep a list of my wrongs.
When I ask for forgiveness
He doesn't pull out a clipboard and say,
"But I've already forgiven him for that
five hundred and sixteen times."
He doesn't remember.

MAX LUCADO

Be strong and courageous.
Do not be afraid...
for the LORD your God goes with you;
he will never leave you nor forsake you.

DEUTERONOMY 31:6

Yes, what joy for those whose record the LORD
has cleared of guilt,
whose lives are lived in complete honesty!

PSALM 32:2 NLT

The voice of sin may be loud,
but the voice of forgiveness is louder.

D. L. MOODY

What was invisible we behold,
What was unknown is known.
Open our eyes to the light of grace,
Unloose our hearts from fear,
Be with us in the strength of love,
Lead us in the hope of courage.

EVELYN FRANCIS CAPEL

Trust God to let you work through this moment
and the next. He will give you all you need.
Don't skip over the painful or confusing moment—
even it has its important and rightful place in the day.

LORD, who may dwell in your sacred tent?
Who may live on your holy mountain?
The one whose walk is blameless,
who does what is righteous,
who speaks the truth from their heart.

PSALM 15:1-2

Faith isn't the absence of fear,
but the courage to walk through it.

Even when I walk through the darkest valley,
I will not be afraid, for you are close beside me.
Your rod and your staff protect and comfort me.

PSALM 23:4 NLT

He did not say, "You will never have a rough passage,
you will never be over-strained,
you will never feel uncomfortable,"
but He did say, "You will never be overcome."

JULIAN OF NORWICH

I know what I'm doing. I have it all planned out—
plans to take care of you, not abandon you,
plans to give you the future you hope for.

JEREMIAH 29:11 MSG

Many promising reconciliations have broken down
because, while both parties came prepared to forgive,
neither party came prepared to be forgiven.

CHARLES WILLIAMS

Courage is the first of human qualities,
because it is the quality which guarantees all others.

WINSTON CHURCHILL

Can we find a friend so faithful,
Who will all our sorrows share?
Jesus knows our every weakness:
Take it to the Lord in prayer.

GEORGE SCRIVEN

God blesses those who are poor and realize
their need for him,
for the Kingdom of Heaven is theirs.
God blesses those who mourn,
for they will be comforted.
God blesses those who are humble,
for they will inherit the whole earth.
God blesses those who hunger and thirst for justice,
for they will be satisfied.
God blesses those who are merciful,
for they will be shown mercy.

MATTHEW 5:3-7 NLT

One person with courage makes a majority.

ANDREW JACKSON

"I love Thee, O LORD, my strength."
The LORD is my rock and my fortress
and my deliverer.
My God, my rock, in whom I take refuge....
For who is God, but the LORD?
And who is a rock, except our God,
The God who girds me with strength
And makes my way blameless?
He makes my feet like hinds' feet
And sets me upon my high places.

PSALM 18:1-2, 31-33 NASB

Have patience with all things,
but chiefly have patience with yourself.
Do not lose courage in considering your own
imperfections but instantly set about remedying
them—every day begin the task anew.

FRANCIS DE SALES

FIVE

The Beauty of Confession

*God grant me the serenity
to accept the things I cannot change;
courage to change the things I can;
and wisdom to know the difference.*

If we admit our sins...he won't let us down;
he'll be true to himself. He'll forgive our sins
and purge us of all wrongdoing.

1 JOHN 1:9 MSG

We need humility to acknowledge our sin.
The knowledge of our sin helps us to rise.
"I will get up and go to my Father."

MOTHER TERESA

I confessed all my sins to you....
And you forgave me! All my guilt is gone.

PSALM 32:5 NLT

Fantastic changes can be made in
feelings with an honest, heart-to-heart talk.
For in the presence of melted hearts
wrongs are forgiven and hurt hearts healed.

DORIS M. MCDOWELL

Hear me as I pray, O LORD.
Be merciful and answer me!
My heart has heard you say, "Come and talk with me."
And my heart responds, "LORD, I am coming."

PSALM 27:7-8 NLT

The serene beauty of a holy life is the most powerful
influence in the world next to the power of God.

BLAISE PASCAL

Lord, hear my voice.
Let your ears be attentive
to my cry for mercy.
If you, LORD, kept a record of sins,
Lord, who could stand?
But with you there is forgiveness,
so that we can, with reverence, serve you.
I wait for the LORD, my whole being waits,
and in his word I put my hope.
I wait for the Lord
more than watchmen wait for the morning....
Put your hope in the LORD,
for with the LORD is unfailing love
and with him is full redemption.

PSALM 130:2–7

We make mistakes, we sin, we fall down,
but each time we get up and begin again.
We pray again. We seek to follow God again....
We confess and begin again...and again...and again.

RICHARD J. FOSTER

When I fall, I will arise; when I sit in darkness,
The LORD will be a light to me.

MICAH 7:8 NKJV

True forgiveness includes total acceptance.
And out of acceptance wounds are healed
and happiness is possible again.

CATHERINE MARSHALL

His names will be: Amazing Counselor, Strong God,
Eternal Father, Prince of Wholeness.
His ruling authority will grow, and there'll be
no limits to the wholeness he brings.

ISAIAH 9:6–7 MSG

Have your heart right with Christ,
and He will visit you often, and so turn weekdays
into Sundays, meals into sacraments,
homes into temples, and earth into heaven.

CHARLES H. SPURGEON

The Lord is not slow in doing what he promised—
the way some people understand slowness.
But God is being patient with you.
He does not want anyone to be lost, but he wants
all people to change their hearts and lives.

2 PETER 3:9 NCV

There is no pillow so soft as a clear conscience.

FRENCH PROVERB

Bring your soul to the Great Physician—exactly
as you are, even and especially at your
worst moment. Simply agree with Him that you are
soul-sick indeed. For it is in such moments that
you will most readily sense His healing presence.

TERESA OF AVILA

Answer me, O LORD, for Your lovingkindness is good;
According to the greatness of Your compassion,
turn to me,
And do not hide Your face from Your servant,
For I am in distress; answer me quickly.
Oh draw near to my soul and redeem it.

PSALM 69:16–18 NASB

God's holy beauty comes near you...and it stirs
your drowsing soul.... He creates in you
the desire to find Him and run after Him—
to follow wherever He leads you, and to press
peacefully against His heart wherever He is.

JOHN OF THE CROSS

Lord, You have searched the deepest recesses
of my heart and mind. I don't need to hide
anything from You or act stronger or more
together than I am. Help me to come
before You with complete transparency,
and grant me a supernatural confidence
that I am safe with You and loved by You.

BETH MOORE

Personal perfection is impossible,
but it is possible to aim for genuineness,
honesty, consistency, and moral purity,
and to frankly acknowledge it when we fail.

SUSAN ALEXANDER YATES

You have searched me, LORD, and you know me.
You know when I sit and when I rise;
you perceive my thoughts from afar...
you are familiar with all my ways.
Before a word is on my tongue
you, LORD, know it completely.

PSALM 139:1-4

A generous and free-minded confession disables
a reproach and disarms an injury.

MICHEL DE MONTAIGNE

Confess your sins to each other
and pray for each other so that you may be healed.
The earnest prayer of a righteous person
has great power and produces wonderful results.

JAMES 5:16 NLT

A good conscience and a good confidence go together.

THOMAS BROOKS

We're not quitters who lose out. Oh, no!
We'll stay with it and survive, trusting all the way.

HEBREWS 10:35-36 MSG

O Lord, you are a great and awesome God!
You always fulfill your covenant
and keep your promises of unfailing love
to those who love you and obey your commands.

DANIEL 9:4 NLT

Go to the effort. Invest the time. Write the letter.
Make the apology. Take the trip. Purchase the gift.
Do it. The seized opportunity renders joy.
The neglected brings regret.

MAX LUCADO

Forgiving and being forgiven are two names
for the same thing. The important thing is that
a discord has been resolved.

C. S. LEWIS

Finally, all of you, be like-minded, be sympathetic, love
one another, be compassionate and humble.
Do not repay evil with evil or insult with insult.
On the contrary, repay evil with blessing, because to
this you were called so that you may inherit a blessing.

1 PETER 3:8–9

Jesus is the God whom we can approach
without pride and before whom
we can humble ourselves without despair.

BLAISE PASCAL

SIX

Create in Me a Clean Heart

God grant me the serenity
to accept the things I cannot change;
courage to change the things I can;
and wisdom to know the difference.

Create in me a pure heart, O God,
and renew a steadfast spirit within me.

PSALM 51:10

When the soul has laid down its faults
at the feet of God, it feels as though it had wings.

EUGENIE DE GUERIN

If you give up your life for me, you will find it.

MATTHEW 10:39 NLT

Whatever your loss, pain,
failure, or brokenness, Jesus Christ
is fully capable of bringing about
change unto full restoration.
Just as His resurrection power brings new life,
His redemption power brings new hope.
He is able, for He's more than a Savior!
He's your Redeemer who promises that He will give
"beauty for ashes, the oil of joy for mourning."

JACK HAYFORD

Hope that is seen is no hope at all.
Who hopes for what they already have?
But if we hope for what we do not yet have,
we wait for it patiently.

ROMANS 8:24-25

Jesus offers us the secret to restructuring our lives
in this chaotic world: our hearts can be changed.

GLORIA GAITHER

So, friends, confirm God's invitation to you,
his choice of you. Don't put it off;
do it now. Do this, and you'll have your life
on a firm footing, the streets paved
and the way wide open into the eternal kingdom
of our Master and Savior, Jesus Christ.

1 PETER 1:10–11 MSG

The great marvel of Jesus Christ's salvation
is that He alters heredity.

OSWALD CHAMBERS

What counts is whether we have been
transformed into a new creation. May God's peace
and mercy be upon all who live by this principle;
they are the new people of God.

GALATIANS 6:15–16 NLT

The sufferings we encounter in life—
even garden-variety sorts of trials—are meant
to help us partake of Christ. For when we enter
the fellowship of His sufferings, God strips us
of our "self-help" mindset. We are forced to our
knees and driven to lean on His grace. Then—and it
seems only then—can God impart His Son's
character to us. In so doing, "we are made like Him."

JONI EARECKSON TADA

"You will seek me and find me when you seek me
with all your heart. I will be found by you," declares
the LORD, "and will bring you back from captivity."

JEREMIAH 29:13-14

The important thing is this:
To be ready at any moment to sacrifice
what we are for what we could become.

CHARLES DUBOIS

If you asked me how God has revealed Himself to me,
I should reply, He reveals Himself as Newness.

CARLO CARRETTO

Peace of conscience, liberty of heart,
the sweetness of abandoning ourselves in the hands
of God...finally, freedom from the fears and insatiable
desires of the times, multiply a hundredfold
the happiness which the true children of God possess
in the midst of their crosses, if they are faithful.

FRANÇOIS FÉNELON

May the words of my mouth and the meditation
of my heart be pleasing to you, O LORD,
my rock and my redeemer.

PSALM 19:14 NLT

To repress a harsh answer, to confess a fault, and to
stop (right or wrong) in the midst of self-defense in
gentle submission, sometimes requires a struggle like
life and death. But these three efforts are the golden
threads with which domestic happiness is woven.

CAROLINE GILMAN

Jesus wants to live His life in you, to look through
your eyes, walk with your feet, love with your heart.

MOTHER TERESA

I have come to know a God
who has a soft spot for rebels,
who recruits people like the adulterer David,
the whiner Jeremiah, the traitor Peter,
and the human-rights abuser Saul of Tarsus.
I have come to know a God whose Son
made prodigals the heroes of His stories
and the trophies of His ministry.

PHILIP YANCEY

When we focus on God, the scene changes.
He's in control of our lives;
nothing lies outside the realm
of His redemptive grace.
Even when we make mistakes,
fail in relationships,
or deliberately make bad choices,
God can redeem us.

PENELOPE STOKES

This is what the LORD says—your Redeemer...
"I am the LORD your God, who teaches you what is best
for you, who directs you in the way you should go."

ISAIAH 48:17

Unceasing Prayer has a way of speaking peace
to the chaos. Our fractured and fragmented
activities begin focusing around a new Center
of Reference. We experience peace, stillness,
serenity, firmness of life orientation.

RICHARD J. FOSTER

Strive for full restoration, encourage one another,
be of one mind, live in peace.
And the God of love and peace will be with you.

2 CORINTHIANS 13:11

The LORD gives strength to his people;
the LORD blesses his people with peace.

PSALM 29:11

Genuine love sees faces, not a mass: the Good
Shepherd "calleth His own sheep by name."

GEORGE A. BUTTRICK

When You said, "Seek My face," my heart said to You,
"Your face, O LORD, I shall seek."

PSALM 27:8 NASB

Gentleness, in its genuine and original meaning...
was a term denoting true inner strength under control.

CHARLES R. SWINDOLL

Blessed are the gentle,
for they shall inherit the earth.

MATTHEW 5:5 NASB

The answer for satisfying living for the Christian
lies not in organizing, managing, or controlling life,
but in focusing life.... Life is simplified
when there is one center, one reason,
one motivation, one direction and purpose.

JEAN FLEMING

Do you not know that in a race all the runners run,
but only one gets the prize? Run in such a way
as to get the prize. Everyone who competes
in the games goes into strict training.
They do it to get a crown that will not last,
but we do it to get a crown that will last forever.

1 CORINTHIANS 9:24-25

SEVEN

Walking Humbly

God grant me the serenity
to accept the things I cannot change;
courage to change the things I can;
and wisdom to know the difference.

LORD, You have heard the desire of the humble;
You will strengthen their heart,
You will incline Your ear.

PSALM 10:17 NASB

We are asked only to be real, trusting in His
perfection to cover our imperfection,
knowing that one day we will finally be
all that Christ saved us for and wants us to be.

GIGI GRAHAM TCHIVIDJIAN

For the LORD takes delight in his people;
he crowns the humble with victory.
Let his faithful people rejoice
in this honor and sing for joy.

PSALM 149:4-5

Humility is strong—not bold;
Quiet—not speechless;
Sure—not arrogant.

ESTELLE SMITH

God's love elevates us without inflating us
and humbles us without degrading us.

B. NOTTAGE

Always be humble and gentle.
Be patient with each other, making allowance
for each other's faults because of your love.

EPHESIANS 4:2 NLT

If the Lord be with us,
we have no cause of fear.
His eye is upon us, His arm over us,
His ear open to our prayer—His grace sufficient,
His promise unchangeable.

JOHN NEWTON

They will rebuild the ancient ruins
and restore the places long devastated;
they will renew the ruined cities
that have been devastated for generations.

ISAIAH 61:4

Through the power of the indwelling Spirit,
we will be able to overcome the sins
that previously mastered us,
and the leading that God will give us
will enable us to find a way through
problems of guidance, self-fulfillment,
[and] heart's desire.

J. I. PACKER

Unless the LORD builds the house,
They labor in vain who build it.

PSALM 127:1 NASB

Everywhere we look the process of transformation
from death to life is seen.
New life is bursting forth all about us.

RAYMOND K. PETRUCCI

God, who said, "Let light shine out of darkness,"
made his light shine in our hearts to give us
the light of the knowledge of God's glory displayed
in the face of Christ. But we have this treasure
in jars of clay to show that this all-surpassing
power is from God and not from us.

2 CORINTHIANS 4:6-7

Not only is God's nature love, but He is also light....
He is against any darkness that may hinder us from
His love producing life and intimacy with Him and
others. The very purpose of light is to set us free
from anything that hinders deeper intimacy with Him.

JACK FROST

Each day brings us a chance
to do better and to make good.

L. BEVAN JONES

Even before he made the world, God loved us
and chose us in Christ to be holy and without fault in
his eyes. God decided in advance to adopt us
into his own family by bringing us to himself
through Jesus Christ. This is what he wanted to do,
and it gave him great pleasure.

EPHESIANS 1:4-5 NLT

A life transformed by the power of God
is always a marvel and a miracle.

GERALDINE NICHOLAS

The life of Jesus is meaningless unless we believe
that He lived, died, and rose again with but one
purpose in mind: to make brand-new creation.
Not to make people with better morals but to create
a community of prophets and professional lovers,
men and women who...would enter into the center
of it all, the very heart and mystery of Christ,
into the center of the flame that consumes,
purifies, and sets everything aglow with peace, joy,
boldness, and extravagant, furious love.

BRENNAN MANNING

Lord...forgive me for thinking pitifully little of the
person You've made me. Forgive me for committing
the flagrant sin of despising myself and considering
myself inferior to others. Forgive me equally
for every time I've sighed with relief at the thought
that I might be superior after all.

BETH MOORE

Humility...creates in us a capacity
for the closest possible intimacy with God.

MONICA BALDWIN

This is my prayer for you: that your love will grow
more and more...that you will be filled
with the good things produced in your life
by Christ to bring glory and praise to God.

PHILIPPIANS 1:9, 11 NCV

There are those who suffer greatly,
and yet, through the recognition that pain
can be a thread in the pattern of God's weaving,
find the way to a fundamental joy.

If Christ lives in us, controlling our personalities,
we will leave glorious marks on the lives
we touch. Not because of our lovely characters,
but because of His.

EUGENIA PRICE

And my God shall supply all your need according
to His riches in glory by Christ Jesus.

PHILIPPIANS 4:19 NKJV

It is right and good that we,
for all things, at all times, and in all places,
give thanks and praise to You, O God.
We worship You, we confess to You, we praise You...
Maker, Nourisher, Guardian,
Healer, Lord, and Father of all.

LANCELOT ANDREWES

Keep company with GOD, get in on the best.
Open up before GOD, keep nothing back;
he'll do whatever needs to be done.

PSALM 37:4-5 MSG

Be still, and in the quiet moments,
listen to the voice of your heavenly Father.
His words can renew your spirit…
no one knows you and your needs like He does.

JANET WEAVER SMITH

God has given both his promise and his oath.
These two things are unchangeable
because it is impossible for God to lie.
Therefore, we who have fled to him
for refuge can have great confidence
as we hold to the hope that lies before us.
This hope is a strong and trustworthy
anchor for our souls.

HEBREWS 6:18–19 NLT

For [God] is, indeed, a wonderful Father
who longs to pour out His mercy upon us,
and whose majesty is so great that
He can transform us from deep within.

TERESA OF AVILA

The precious truth of Jesus' power as Redeemer
is that He has a plan and an ability to progressively
restore the broken parts of human experience
and to reproduce a whole person.

JACK HAYFORD

Keep on asking, and you will receive what you ask for.
Keep on seeking, and you will find. Keep on knocking,
and the door will be opened to you.

MATTHEW 7:7 NLT

Faith is meant to be lived moment by moment.
It isn't some broad, general outline—it's a long walk
with a real Person. Details count: Passing thought,
small sacrifices, a few encouraging words, little acts
of kindness, brief victories over nagging sins.

JONI EARECKSON TADA

He guides the humble in what is right
and teaches them his way.

PSALM 25:9

God is a Transformer like no other,
taking my sin-scarred soul and transforming
me into a brand-new showpiece of His grace.

Where the Spirit of the Lord is,
there is freedom. And we all,
who with unveiled faces
contemplate the Lord's glory,
are being transformed into
his image with ever-increasing glory,
which comes from the Lord, who is the Spirit.

2 CORINTHIANS 3:17-18

The Word of God, Jesus Christ, on account
of His great love for mankind, became what we are
in order to make us what He is Himself.

IRENAEUS

We are transfigured much like the Messiah,
our lives gradually becoming brighter
and more beautiful as God enters
our lives and we become like him.

1 CORINTHIANS 3:16 MSG

EIGHT

Peace and Honor

God grant me the serenity
to accept the things I cannot change;
courage to change the things I can,
and wisdom to know the difference.

Do things in such a way that everyone can see
you are honorable. Do all that you can
to live in peace with everyone.

ROMANS 12:17–18 NLT

By living fully, recognizing that all we do
is by His [God's] power, we honor Him;
He in turn blesses us.

BECKY LAIRD

Anyone united with the Messiah gets a fresh start,
is created new. The old life is gone;
a new life burgeons! Look at it!
All this comes from the God who settled
the relationship between us and him, and then called
us to settle our relationships with each other.

2 CORINTHIANS 5:17–18 MSG

Don't be discouraged by a failure.
It can be a positive experience.
Failure is, in a sense, the highway to success,
inasmuch as every discovery of what is false
leads us to seek earnestly after what is true,
and every fresh experience points out some form
of error which we shall afterwards carefully avoid.

JOHN KEATS

God's will is doing those things we know to be right
for each day and doing them the best we possibly can.

GLORIA GAITHER

So don't you see that we don't owe this old do-it-
yourself life one red cent. There's nothing in it for us,
nothing at all. The best thing to do is give it a decent
burial and get on with your new life. God's Spirit
beckons. There are things to do and places to go!

ROMANS 8:12 MSG

The remarkable truth is that our choices matter,
not just to us and our own destiny but, amazingly,
to God Himself and the universe He rules.

PHILIP YANCEY

If you keep yourself pure, you will be a special utensil
for honorable use. Your life will be clean,
and you will be ready for the Master to use you
for every good work.

2 TIMOTHY 2:21 NLT

My dear brothers and sisters,
stand firm. Let nothing move you.
Always give yourselves fully
to the work of the Lord,
because you know that your
labor in the Lord is not in vain.

1 CORINTHIANS 15:58

Our God is a God who not merely restores,
but takes up our mistakes and follies
into His plan for us and brings good out of them.

J. I. PACKER

Restore us, O God; make your face
shine on us, that we may be saved....
Then we will not turn away from you;
revive us, and we will call on your name.
Restore us, LORD God Almighty; make your face
shine on us, that we may be saved.

PSALM 80:3, 18

I have satiated the weary soul,
and I have replenished every sorrowful soul.

JEREMIAH 31:25 NKJV

Jesus is the Savior, but He is even more than that!
He is more than a Forgiver of our sins.
He is even more than our Provider of eternal life.
He is our Redeemer! He is the One who is ready
to recover and restore what the power of sin
and death has taken from us.

JACK HAYFORD

Nothing in the world
can take the place of persistence.

CALVIN COOLIDGE

The LORD is my shepherd, I shall not want.
He makes me lie down in green pastures,
He leads me beside quiet waters, He restores my soul.

PSALM 23:1-3 NASB

And the ransomed of the LORD will return
And come with joyful shouting to Zion,
With everlasting joy upon their heads
They will find gladness and joy
And sorrow and sighing will flee away.

ISAIAH 35:10 NASB

Let's praise His name! He is holy,
He is almighty, He is love. He brings hope,
forgiveness, heart cleansing, peace and power.
He is our deliverer and coming King.
Praise His wonderful name!

LUCILLE M. LAW

Remember, O LORD,
your compassion and unfailing love,
which you have shown from long ages past.
Do not remember the rebellious sins of my youth.
Remember me in the light of your unfailing love,
for you are merciful, O LORD.

PSALM 25:6–7 NLT

But now, this is what the LORD says—
he who created you...
"Do not fear, for I have redeemed you;
I have summoned you by name; you are mine.
When you pass through the waters,
I will be with you;
and when you pass through the rivers,
they will not sweep over you.
When you walk through the fire,
you will not be burned;
the flames will not set you ablaze.
For I am the LORD your God,
the Holy One of Israel, your Savior.

ISAIAH 43:1-3 NIV

People, even more than things, have to be restored,
renewed, revived, reclaimed and redeemed.

SAM LEVENSON

Grace, like water, flows to the lowest part.

PHILIP YANCEY

It is God who works in you both
to will and to do for His good pleasure.

PHILIPPIANS 2:13 NKJV

Oddly, the most freeing thing we can ever do is to
abdicate the throne of our own miniature kingdoms.

BETH MOORE

"I desire to do your will, my God;
your law is within my heart."
...I speak of your faithfulness and your saving help.

PSALM 40:8, 10

Father...I will accept Your will, whatever that may
be. Thank you for counting this act of my will as the
decision of the real person even when my emotions
protest.... It is You, Lord God, who alone are worthy
of worship, I bend the knee with thanksgiving
that this too will "work together for good."

CATHERINE MARSHALL

My health may fail, and my spirit may grow weak,
but God remains the strength of my heart;
he is mine forever

PSALM 73:26 NLT

NINE

Loving Others

*God grant me the serenity
to accept the things I cannot change;
courage to change the things I can;
and wisdom to know the difference.*

Above all, clothe yourselves with love,
which binds us all together in perfect harmony.

COLOSSIANS 3:14 NLT

Sometimes it is necessary for us to speak.
At other times it is important that we be quiet.
Wisdom comes with knowing the difference.

MRS. D. E. CLAY

The wisdom from above is first of all pure.
It is also peace loving, gentle at all times,
and willing to yield to others.
It is full of mercy and good deeds.
It shows no favoritism and is always sincere.

JAMES 3:17 NLT

If I speak in the tongues of men or of angels,
but do not have love, I am only a resounding
gong or a clanging cymbal.

1 CORINTHIANS 13:1

Often we have no choice about doing things,
but we can always choose how to do them.
And that...can make all the difference
in your daily life.

NORMAN VINCENT PEALE

Change that which can be altered,
explain that which can be understood,
teach that which can be learned,
resolve that which can be settled,
and negotiate that which is open to compromise.

JAMES DOBSON

There is a time for everything, and everything
on earth has its special season....
There is a time to be silent and a time to speak.

ECCLESIASTES 3:1, 7 NCV

And since I have no gold to give,
And love alone must make amends,
My only prayer is, while I live—
God make me worthy of my friends.

SHERMAN

If I give all I possess to the poor
and give over my body to hardship that I may boast,
but do not have love, I gain nothing.

1 CORINTHIANS 13:3

No creature that deserved redemption
would need to be redeemed.

C. S. LEWIS

If you enter your place of worship and,
about to make an offering, you suddenly remember
a grudge a friend has against you,
abandon your offering, leave immediately,
go to this friend and make things right.
Then and only then, come back
and work things out with God. Or say you're out
on the street and an old enemy accosts you.
Don't lose a minute. Make the first move;
make things right with him.

MATTHEW 5:23-25 MSG

When we trade with God
we always come out a winner.
Give Him your heart of stone
and He will give you in return, a heart of flesh—
one that is clean and filled with His love.

Walk in a manner worthy of the calling with which
you have been called, with all humility
and gentleness...being diligent to preserve
the unity of the Spirit in the bond of peace.

EPHESIANS 1:1–3 NASB

Great works do not always lie our way,
but every moment we may do little ones excellently,
that is, with great love.

FRANCIS DE SALES

The reason we can dare to risk loving others is that
"God has for Christ's sake loved us." Think of it!
We are loved eternally, totally, individually,
unreservedly! Nothing can take God's love away.

GLORIA GAITHER

God put his love on the line for us
by offering his Son in sacrificial death
while we were of no use whatever to him.

ROMANS 5:8 MSG

Lord, make me an instrument of Thy peace.
Where there is hatred, let me sow love;
Where there is injury, pardon;
Where there is doubt, faith;
Where there is despair, hope;
Where there is darkness, light;
Where there is sadness, joy.
Grant that I may not so much seek
To be consoled as to console,
To be understood as to understand,
To be loved as to love.
For it is in giving that we receive,
It is in pardoning that we are pardoned,
And it is in dying that we are born to eternal life.

FRANCIS OF ASSISI

Love each other deeply with all your heart.

1 PETER 1:22 NLT

Peace of conscience is
nothing but the echo of pardoning mercy.

WILLIAM GURNALL

Our love to God is measured by our everyday
fellowship with others and the love it displays.

ANDREW MURRAY

Kindness is more important than wisdom, and the
recognition of this is the beginning of wisdom.

THEODORE ISAAC RUBIN

My little children, let us not love in word
or in tongue, but in deed and in truth.
And by this we know that we are of the truth,
and shall assure our hearts before Him.

1 JOHN 3:18–19 NKJV

Love is patient, love is kind.
It does not envy, it does not boast,
it is not proud. It does not dishonor others,
it is not self-seeking, it is not easily angered,
it keeps no record of wrongs.

1 CORINTHIANS 13:4–5

Define yourself radically as one beloved by God.
This is the true self. Every other identity is illusion.

BRENNAN MANNING

Just as the Father has loved Me,
I have loved you; abide in My love.

JOHN 15:9 NASB

"Come now, and let us reason together,"
says the LORD, "though your sins are as scarlet,
they will be as white as snow, though they
are red like crimson, they will be like wool."

ISAIAH 1:18 NASB

I need not lack now any more
For any lovely thing;
I need to know my birthright for
My Father is the King!

EVELYN GAGE BROWN

Love...rejoices with the truth. It always protects,
always trusts, always hopes, always perseveres.

1 CORINTHIANS 13:6-7

From God, great and small, rich and poor,
draw living water from a living spring,
and those who serve Him freely and gladly
will receive grace answering to grace.

THOMAS À KEMPIS

So don't lose a minute in building on what you've
been given, complementing your basic faith
with good character, spiritual understanding,
alert discipline, passionate patience, reverent wonder,
warm friendliness, and generous love,
each dimension fitting into and developing the others.

2 PETER 1:5–9 MSG

He who breathes into our hearts
the heavenly hope, will not deceive or fail us
when we press forward to its realization.

L. B. COWMAN

For we are God's handiwork,
created in Christ Jesus to do good works,
which God prepared in advance for us to do.

EPHESIANS 2:10

Forgiveness is man's deepest need
and highest achievement.

HORACE BUSHNELL

Be imitators of God, as beloved children;
and walk in love, just as Christ also loved you
and gave Himself up for us, an offering
and sacrifice to God as a fragrant aroma.

EPHESIANS 5:1–2 NASB

Accept the pain, cherish the joys, resolve the regrets;
then can come the best of benedictions.

JOAN MCINTOSH

I pray that Christ will live in your hearts
by faith and that your life will be strong in love
and be built on love.

EPHESIANS 3:17 NCV

How could I be anything but quite happy
if I believed always that all the past is forgiven,
and all the present furnished with power,
and all the future bright with hope.

JAMES SMETHAM

TEN

Heart Dedication

*God grant me the serenity
to accept the things I cannot change;
courage to change the things I can;
and wisdom to know the difference.*

I have chosen the way of faithfulness;
I have set my heart on your laws.

PSALM 119: 30

The price of success is hard work,
dedication to the job at hand, and the determination
that whether we win or lose, we have applied
the best of ourselves to the task at hand.

VINCENT T. LOMBARDI

I will praise you, Lord my God, with all my heart;
I will glorify your name forever.

PSALM 86:12

For God Himself works in our souls, in their
deepest depths, taking increasing control as we are
progressively willing to be prepared for His wonder.

THOMAS R. KELLY

Be sure to fear the LORD and serve him
faithfully with all your heart;
consider what great things he has done for you.

1 SAMUEL 12:24

God, with all His giving heart,
can only give us Himself as we recognize
the depth of the need in our own lives.

EUGENIA PRICE

[Trials] may come in abundance.
But they cannot penetrate into the sanctuary
of the soul when it is settled in God,
and we may dwell in perfect peace.

HANNAH WHITALL SMITH

I have told you these things,
so that in me you may have peace.
In this world you will have trouble.
But take heart! I have overcome the world.

JOHN 16:33

God looks at the world through the eyes of love.
If we, therefore, as human beings
made in the image of God also want to see
reality rationally, that is, as it truly is,
then we, too, must learn to look at
what we see with love.

ROBERTA BONDI

And now these three remain:
faith, hope and love.
But the greatest of these is love.

1 CORINTHIANS 13:13

If you have succeeded in getting hold of Almighty
God's hand, don't let it go. Keep hold of Him by
constantly renewing...prayers to Him, acts of desire,
and the seeking to please Him in little things.

MOTHER FRANCIS RAPHAEL

Do the things that show you really
have changed your hearts and lives.

MATTHEW 3:8 NCV

It is in the very act of prayer itself—
the intimate, ongoing interaction with God—
that wrong motives are cared for in due time.

RICHARD J. FOSTER

If you think you are standing strong, be careful not
to fall. The temptations in your life are no different
from what others experience. And God is faithful.
He will not allow the temptation to be more
than you can stand. When you are tempted,
he will show you a way out so that you can endure.

1 CORINTHIANS 10:12–13 NLT

From the heart of God comes
the strongest rhythm—the rhythm of love.
Without His love reverberating in us,
whatever we do will come across like a noisy gong
or a clanging cymbal. And so the work
of the human heart, it seems to me, is to listen
for that music and pick up on its rhythms.

KEN GIRE

But what happens when we live God's way?
He brings gifts into our lives,
much the same way that fruit appears
in an orchard— things like affection for others,
exuberance about life, serenity.
We develop...a sense of compassion in the heart.

GALATIANS 5:22 MSG

What you promise today must be renewed
and redecided tomorrow and each day
that stretches out before you.

ARTHUR GORDON

What will happen to those whose longing
for God is...intense? Jesus promises,
"they shall be satisfied...." We will become
so spiritually satisfied that we will be...strong,
stable, able to handle harsh conditions
and endure uncomfortable circumstances.
Now that's a needed promise!
God's pantry never runs low. His wells never run dry.

CHARLES R. SWINDOLL

The master answered, "You did well. You are a good
and loyal servant. Because you were loyal with small
things, I will let you care for much greater things.
Come and share my joy with me."

MATTHEW 25:23 NCV

When you see God face to face, he's not going to hold
you accountable for the entire world. But He will hold
you accountable for what was entrusted to you.

PAUL MEIER

The abiding presence of the Savior from sin
is promised to all who have accepted Him
in the fullness of His redeeming power,
and who preach by their lives as well as by their words
what a wonderful Savior He is.

ANDREW MURRAY

"I am the LORD who exercises lovingkindness,
justice and righteousness on earth;
for I delight in these things," declares the LORD.

JEREMIAH 9:24 NASB

God's Word acts as a light for our paths.
It can help scare off unwanted thoughts in our minds
and protect us from the enemy.

GARY SMALLEY AND JOHN TRENT

We capture every thought
and make it give up and obey Christ.

2 CORINTHIANS 10:5 NCV

In the cellar of your heart lurk the ghosts
of yesterday's sins. Sins you've confessed;
errors of which you've repented; damage you've
done your best to repair.... Do yourself a favor.
Purge your cellar. Exorcise your basement.
Take the Roman nails of Calvary and board
up the door. And remember...He forgot.

MAX LUCADO

Praise the LORD, my soul,
and forget not all his benefits—
who forgives all your sins and heals all your diseases,
who redeems your life from the pit
and crowns you with love and compassion....
For as high as the heavens are above the earth,
so great is his love for those who fear him;
as far as the east is from the west,
so far has he removed our transgressions from us.

PSALM 103:2-4, 11-12

Swim through your temptations and troubles.
Run to the promises, they [are] our Lord's branches
hanging over the water so that His...children may
take a grip of them.

SAMUEL RUTHERFORD

A pharisee is hard on others and easy on himself,
but a spiritual man is easy on others
and hard on himself.

A. W. TOZER

Help us, O Lord,
when we want to do the right thing,
but know not what it is.
But help us most when we know perfectly well
what we ought to do, and do not want to do it.

PETER MARSHALL

I hold on to you for dear life,
and you hold me steady as a post.

PSALM 63:5 MSG

When we walk with the Lord in the light of the Word,
what a glory He sheds on our way!
While we do His good will He abides with us still,
and with all who will trust and obey.

JOHN STAMMIS

You enlarged my path under me,
So my feet did not slip.

PSALM 18:36 NKJV

O Lord, give us a mind that is humble,
quiet, peaceable, patient and charitable,
and a taste of Your Holy Spirit
in all our thoughts, words, and deeds.
O Lord, give us a lively faith, a firm hope,
a fervent charity, a love of You.
Take from us all lukewarmness in meditation
and all dullness in prayer.
Give us fervor and delight in thinking of You,
Your grace, and Your tender compassion toward us.
Give us, good Lord, the grace to work for
the things we pray for.

THOMAS MORE

Love is the strongest force in the world,
and when it is blocked that means pain.
There are two things we can do when this happens.
We can kill the love so that it stops hurting.
But then of course part of us dies, too.
Or...we can ask God to open up
another route for that love to travel.

CASPER TEN BOOM

Now may God himself, the God of peace, make you
pure, belonging only to him. May your whole self—
spirit, soul, and body—be kept safe and without fault
when our Lord Jesus Christ comes. You can trust
the One who calls you to do that for you.

1 THESSALONIANS 5:23–24 NCV

I want first of all...to be at peace with myself,
I want a singleness of eye, a purity of intention,
a central core to my life.... I want, in fact—to borrow
from the language of the saints—to live "in grace"
as much of the time as possible.

ANNE MORROW LINDBERGH

A saint is never consciously a saint;
a saint is consciously dependent on God.

OSWALD CHAMBERS

May the Lord direct your hearts into the love of God
and into the steadfastness of Christ.

2 THESSALONIANS 3:5 NASB

May Jesus himself and God our Father,
who reached out in love and surprised you
with gifts of unending help and confidence,
put a fresh heart in you, invigorate your work,
enliven your speech.

2 THESSALONIANS 2:15 MSG

If you would reap praise, sow the seeds:
Gentle words and useful deeds.

FRANCIS DE SALES

Our conscience testifies that we have conducted
ourselves in the world, and especially in our relations
with you, with integrity and godly sincerity.
We have done so, relying not on worldly wisdom
but on God's grace.

2 CORINTHIANS 1:12

Grace on display: when He gently washed the feet
of one who would walk out and betray Him in the end.

ELEVEN

Drawing Near

*God grant me the serenity
to accept the things I cannot change;
courage to change the things I can;
and wisdom to know the difference.*

Draw near to God
and He will draw near to you.

JAMES 4:8 NASB

Life in the presence of God
should be known to us in conscious experience.
It is a life to be enjoyed every moment of every day.

A. W. TOZER

May you be filled with joy, always thanking the Father.
He has enabled you to share in the inheritance
that belongs to his people, who live in the light.

COLOSSIANS 1:11-12 NLT

We are God's fellow workers, and as such we turn
to prayer to equip us for the partnership.

PHILIP YANCEY

[God] will never let you be shaken
or moved from your place near His heart.

JONI EARECKSON

He must become greater and greater,
and I must become less and less.

JOHN 3:30 NLT

Your life is a journey you must travel
with a deep consciousness of God.

1 PETER 1:18 MSG

Every day we live is a priceless gift of God,
loaded with possibilities to learn something new,
to gain fresh insights.

DALE EVANS ROGERS

May you have the power to understand,
as all God's people should, how wide, how long,
how high, and how deep his love is.
May you experience the love of Christ,
though it is too great to understand fully.
Then you will be made complete with all the fullness
of life and power that comes from God.

EPHESIANS 3:18–19 NLT

All the things in this world are gifts and signs of God's
love to us. The whole world is a love letter from God.

PETER KREEFT

I am an eternal being, created by God.
I am an individual with purpose. It's not what I get
from life, but who I am, that makes the difference.

NEVA COYLE

I pray that from his glorious, unlimited resources
he will empower you with inner strength through
his Spirit. Then Christ will make his home in your
hearts as you trust in him. Your roots will grow
down into God's love and keep you strong.

EPHESIANS 3:16–17 NLT

When peace like a river attendeth my way,
When sorrows like sea billows roll;
Whatever my lot, Thou hast taught me to say,
"It is well, it is well with my soul...."

HORATIO G. SPAFFORD

He has redeemed my soul in peace
from the battle that was against me.

PSALM 55:18 NKJV

In the morning let our hearts gaze upon God's love
and the love He has allowed us to share, and in the
beauty of that vision, let us go forth to meet the day.

ROY LESSIN

His divine power has given us everything
we need for a godly life through our knowledge
of him who called us by his own glory and goodness.

2 PETER 1:3

As we practice the presence of God,
more and more we find ourselves
going through the stresses and strains
of daily activity with an ease and serenity
that amaze even us...especially us.

RICHARD J. FOSTER

Let all that I am wait quietly before God,
for my hope is in him.
He alone is my rock and my salvation.

PSALM 62:5-6 NLT

His will is our hiding place. Lord Jesus, keep me in your
will! Don't let me go mad by poking about outside of it!

CORRIE TEN BOOM

A day in Your courts is better than a thousand
outside.... For the LORD God is a sun and shield;
the LORD gives grace and glory; no good thing
does He withhold from those who walk uprightly.

PSALM 84:10-11 NASB

People who pray are no more saints
than the rest of us. Rather, they are people
who want to share a life with God,
to love and be loved, to speak and to listen,
to work and to be at rest in the presence of God.

ROBERTA BONDI

How precious to me are your thoughts, God!
How vast is the sum of them!
Were I to count them,
they would outnumber the grains of sand—
when I awake, I am still with you.

PSALM 139:17-18

There is no mode of life in the world
more pleasing and more full of delight
than continual conversation with God.

BROTHER LAWRENCE

Prayer changes things, but it also changes us.
In the very act of prayer, we open ourselves
to the will of another—God.

GLORIA GAITHER

Do not conform to the pattern of this world,
but be transformed by the renewing of your mind.
Then you will be able to test and approve
what God's will is—his good, pleasing and perfect will.

ROMANS 12:2

I'll go where You want me to go, dear Lord,
O'er mountain, or plain, or sea;
I'll say what You want me to say, dear Lord,
I'll be what You want me to be.

MARY BROWN

If you abide in Me, and My words abide in you,
you will ask what you desire,
and it shall be done for you.

JOHN 15:7 NKJV

So wait before the Lord. Wait in the stillness.
And In that stillness, assurance will come to you.
You will know that you are heard; you will know that
your Lord ponders the voice of your humble desires;
you will hear quiet words spoken to you yourself,
perhaps to your grateful surprise and refreshment.

AMY CARMICHAEL

For the word of the LORD holds true,
and we can trust everything he does.
He loves whatever is just and good;
the unfailing love of the LORD fills the earth.
The LORD merely spoke, and the heavens
were created. He breathed the word,
and all the stars were born.

PSALM 33:4-6 NLT

Wait for the LORD; be strong and let your heart
take courage; yes, wait for the LORD.

PSALM 27:14 NASB

The Bible extols waiting,
partly because it requires qualities
which the Lord wants to encourage in us,
like patience, which I need so badly.
But there is another reason too. Waiting works.
It is a joining of man and God to achieve an end,
and the end is always a form of the Easter story.

CATHERINE MARSHALL

You're my place of quiet retreat;
I wait for your Word to renew me....
Therefore I lovingly embrace everything you say.

PSALM 119:114, 119 MSG

Prayer imparts the power to walk and not faint.

OSWALD CHAMBERS

Being able to bow in prayer
as the day begins or ends gives expression
to the frustrations and concerns
that might not otherwise be ventilated.
On the other end of that prayer line
is a loving heavenly Father who has promised
to hear and answer our petitions.

JAMES DOBSON

Humble yourselves, therefore, under God's mighty
hand, that he may lift you up in due time.
Cast all your anxiety on him because he cares for you.

1 PETER 5:6-7

The possibilities of prayer run parallel
with the promises of God. Prayer opens an outlet
for the promises...and secures their precious ends.

E. M. BOUNDS

Prayer is the serious, thoughtful, persistent endeavor
to put our lives at the service of the best.

FREDERICK ELIOT

How slow we are to believe in God as God,
sovereign, all-seeing and almighty!
We need to "wait upon the Lord" in meditations
on His majesty, till we find our strength renewed
through the writing of these things upon our hearts.

J. I. PACKER

Those who wait on the LORD
Shall renew their strength;
They shall mount up with wings like eagles.

ISAIAH 40:31 NKJV

Twant me, 'twas the Lord. I always told Him,
"I trust to You. I don't know where to go or what to
do, but I expect You to lead me," and He always did.

HARRIET TUBMAN

Hear my cry for help, my King and my God,
for to you I pray. In the morning, LORD,
you hear my voice; in the morning I lay my requests
before you and wait expectantly.

PSALM 5:2-3

Do you know that nothing you do in this life
will ever matter, unless it is about loving God
and loving the people He has made?

FRANCIS CHAN

God, sometimes Your smallest creatures
have the largest hearts. Help me do unto others
with a larger heart.

EDWARD GRINNAN

I run in the path of your commands,
for you have broadened my understanding.
Teach me, LORD, the way of your decrees,
that I may follow it to the end.
Give me understanding,
so that I may keep your law
and obey it with all my heart

PSALM 119:32-34

God saved us and called us to live a holy life.
He did this, not because we deserved it,
but because that was his plan from
before the beginning of time—
to show us his grace through Christ Jesus.

2 TIMOTHY 1:9 NLT

Give me a pure heart—that I may see Thee.
A humble heart—that I may hear Thee.
A heart of love—that I may serve Thee.
A heart of faith—that I may abide in Thee.

DAG HAMMARSKJÖLD

Prayer and [God's] Word are inseparably
linked together.... The Word gives me guidance
for prayer, telling me what God will do for me.
It gives me the power to pray, telling me how God
would have me come.... Prayer seeks God; the Word
reveals God. In prayer we rise to heaven to dwell
with God; in the Word God comes to dwell with us.

ANDREW MURRAY

Seek the LORD while he may be found;
call on him while he is near....
Turn to the LORD, and he will have mercy...
and to our God, for he will freely pardon.

ISAIAH 55:6-7

He is most glorified in us
when we are most satisfied in Him.

JOHN PIPER

As white snowflakes fall quietly
and thickly on a winter day, answers to prayer
will settle down upon you at every step you take,
even to your dying day. The story of your life
will be the story of prayer and answers to prayer.

OLE HALLESBY

The counsel of the LORD stands forever,
The plans of His heart from generation to generation.

PSALM 33:11 NASB

Often I have made a request of God
with earnest pleadings even backed up
with Scripture, only to have Him say "No"
because He had something better in store.

RUTH BELL GRAHAM

As it is written: "What no eye has seen,
what no ear has heard, and what no human mind
has conceived"—the things God has prepared
for those who love him.

1 CORINTHIANS 2:9

TWELVE

Keeping the Faith

*God grant me the serenity
to accept the things I cannot change;
courage to change the things I can;
and wisdom to know the difference.*

The life I now live...I live by faith in the Son of God,
who loved me and gave himself for me.

GALATIANS 2:20

Therefore, since we have a great high priest
who has ascended into heaven,
Jesus the Son of God, let us hold firmly
to the faith we profess. For we do not have
a high priest who is unable to empathize
with our weaknesses, but we have one
who has been tempted in every way,
just as we are—yet he did not sin.

HEBREWS 4:14-15

When God has become our shepherd,
our refuge, our fortress, then we can reach out
to Him in the midst of a broken world
and feel at home while still on the way.

HENRI J. M. NOUWEN

I am only a small container of Your Spirit, Lord.
Let others be affected by the spill-over.

NEVA COYLE

The overflowing life does not just happen.
It is only as our own deep thirst is quenched, only
as we are filled ourselves, that we can be channels
through which His overflow reaches other lives.

GRACE STRICKER DAWSON

On the day I called, You answered me;
You made me bold with strength in my soul

PSALM 138:3 NASB

I will sing of the LORD's great love forever;
with my mouth I will make your faithfulness known
through all generations. I will declare that your love
stands firm forever, that you have established your
faithfulness in heaven itself.

PSALM 89:1-2

Every day we meet people whose eternal destiny
may be affected by what we do or say.

JANETTE OKE

God's gifts and God's call are under full warranty—
never canceled, never rescinded.

ROMANS 11:29 MSG

Allow your dreams a place in your prayers and plans.
God-given dreams can help you move into the future
He is preparing for you.

BARBARA JOHNSON

There are vast, untapped resources of faith...
and talent...that can only be discovered in adversity.

ROBERT SCHULLER

The LORD will perfect that which concerns me;
Your mercy, O LORD, endures forever.

PSALM 138:8 NKJV

Let us examine our capacities and gifts,
and then put them to the best use we may....
God can do great things with our lives,
if we but give them to Him in sincerity.

ANNA R. B. LINDSAY

I pray that God, the source of hope,
will fill you completely with joy and peace
because you trust in him. Then you will
overflow with confident hope
through the power of the Holy Spirit.

ROMANS 15:13 NLT

His overflowing love delights to make us partakers
of the bounties He graciously imparts.

HANNAH MORE

I have come that they may have life,
and have it to the full.

JOHN 10:10

The Creator thinks enough of you to have sent
Someone very special so that you might have life—
abundantly, joyfully, completely, and victoriously.

He who began a good work in you will carry it on
to completion until the day of Christ Jesus.

PHILIPPIANS 1:6

Look back from where we have come....
How could we know the joy without the suffering?
And how could we endure the suffering but that
we are warmed and carried on the breast of God?

DESMOND M. TUTU

One thing I have asked from the LORD,
that I shall seek:
That I may dwell in the house of the LORD
all the days of my life,
To behold the beauty of the LORD
And to meditate in His temple.
For in the day of trouble He will
conceal me in His tabernacle;
In the secret place of His tent He will hide me;
He will lift me up on a rock.

PSALM 27:4–5 NASB

By putting the gift of yearning for God
into every human being's heart, God at the same time
draws all people made in God's image to God's self
and into their own true selves.

ROBERTA BONDI

The best thing about the future
is that it comes only one day at a time.

ABRAHAM LINCOLN

Praise be to the Lord, to God our Savior,
who daily bears our burdens.

PSALM 68:19

Lord...give me the gift of faith to be renewed
and shared with others each day.
Teach me to live this moment only,
looking neither to the past with regret,
nor the future with apprehension.
Let love be my aim and my life a prayer.

ROSEANN ALEXANDER-ISHAM

I focus on this one thing: Forgetting the past
and looking forward to what lies ahead,
I press on to reach the end of the race
and receive the heavenly prize for which God,
through Christ Jesus, is calling us.

PHILIPPIANS 3:13-14 NLT

In Love's service, only wounded soldiers can serve.

BRENNAN MANNING

The Spirit of the Lord GOD is upon Me,
Because the LORD has anointed Me
To preach good tidings to the poor;
He has sent Me to heal the brokenhearted,
To proclaim liberty to the captives,
And the opening of the prison to those
who are bound...
To comfort all who mourn,
To console those who mourn in Zion,
To give them beauty for ashes,
The oil of joy for mourning,
The garment of praise for the spirit of heaviness;
That they may be called trees of righteousness,
The planting of the LORD, that He may be glorified.

ISAIAH 61:1-3 NKJV

God's work done in God's way
will never lack God's supply.

HUDSON TAYLOR

One of the most poisonous of all Satan's whispers
is simply, "Things will never change."
That lie kills expectation, trapping our heart forever
in the present. To keep desire alive and flourishing,
we must renew our vision for what lies ahead....
Jesus has promised to "make all things new."

JOHN ELDREDGE

He will also keep you firm to the end,
so that you will be blameless on the day of our Lord
Jesus Christ. God is faithful, who has called you into
fellowship with his Son, Jesus Christ our Lord.

1 CORINTHIANS 1:8–10

Let the redeemed of the LORD tell their story—
those he redeemed from the hand of the foe....
Let them give thanks to the LORD
for his unfailing love
and his wonderful deeds for mankind,
for he satisfies the thirsty
and fills the hungry with good things.

PSALM 107:2, 8–9

True prayer is simply a quiet, sincere,
genuine conversation with God.
It is a two-way dialogue between friends.

W. PHILIP KELLER

The fruit of that righteousness will be peace;
its effect will be quietness and confidence forever.

ISAIAH 32:17 NIV

Perhaps today your burden is greater
than your capacity.
Tell the Lord, for He will
either lighten the load or,
by His power, increase your capacity
to bear the burden.

NONA KELLEY

Come to Me, all who are weary and heavy-laden,
and I will give you rest. Take My yoke upon you
and learn from Me, for I am gentle and humble
in heart, and you will find rest for your souls.

MATTHEW 11:28-29 NASB

Prayer is not a means of removing the unknown
and predictable elements in life, but rather a way
of including the unknown and unpredictable in the
outworking of the grace of God in our lives.

PHILIP YANCEY

How precious is your unfailing love, O God!
All humanity finds shelter in the shadow of your wings.
You feed them from the abundance of your own
house, letting them drink from your river of delights.

PSALM 36:7-8 NLT

Jesus knows when a request comes to Him
from the heart. He has been waiting all along
for us to bring our needy selves to Him
and receive from Him that eternal water.

DORIS GAILEY

We know that in all things God works
for the good of those who love him,
who have been called according to his purpose.

ROMANS 8:28

Over and over Jesus implores His followers,
"Take courage!" as if His hand is outstretched
and His palm opened with offered treasure.
It's time we took Him up on it.

BETH MOORE

"For the mountains may be removed
and the hills may shake,
But My lovingkindness will not be removed from you,
And My covenant of peace will not be shaken,"
Says the LORD who has compassion on you.

ISAIAH 54:10 NASB

No need to panic over alarms
or surprises, or predictions
that doomsday's just around the corner,
Because GOD will be right there with you;
he'll keep you safe and sound.

PROVERBS 3:26 MSG

Remember that you are needed.
There is at least one important work to be done
that will not be done unless you do it.

CHARLES ALLEN

Each of you should use whatever
gift you have received to serve others,
as faithful stewards of God's grace
in its various forms. If anyone speaks,
they should do so as one who speaks
the very words of God. If anyone serves,
they should do so with the strength
God provides, so that in all things
God may be praised through Jesus Christ.

1 PETER 4:10-11

To live in prayer together is to walk in love together.

MARGARET JACOBS

Our words can promote growth
by wrapping others in a cocoon of love and hope.

GARY SMALLEY AND JOHN TRENT

When someone else knows and cares,
then we pay that much more attention
to what we're doing.

TILDEN H. EDWARDS

Tuck [this] thought into your heart today.
Treasure it. Your Father God cares about
your daily everythings that concern you.

KAY ARTHUR

For the LORD your God is living among you.
He is a mighty savior. He will take delight in you
with gladness. With his love, he will calm all your
fears. He will rejoice over you with joyful songs.

ZEPHANIAH 3:17 NLT

The King of love my Shepherd is,
Whose goodness faileth never;
I nothing lack if I am His,
And He is mine forever.

SIR HENRY WILLIAMS BAKER

This is how much God loved the world:
he gave his Son, his one and only Son.
And this is why: so that no one need
be destroyed; by believing in him,
anyone can have a whole and lasting life.

JOHN 3:16 MSG

I know whom I have believed
and am persuaded that He is able to keep
what I have committed to Him until that Day.

2 TIMOTHY 1:12 NKJV

Faith is not exactly belief. One can believe
anything...it's an assent in the mind.
But faith is completely different. It's the actual
active *engagement* of *God* in one's personal life.

BRIAN STILLER

At the very heart and foundation
of all God's dealings with us...we must dare
to believe in and assert the infinite,
unmerited, and unchanging love of God.

L. B. COWMAN

You prepare a table before me in the presence
of my enemies; you anoint my head with oil;
my cup runs over. Surely goodness and mercy
shall follow me all the days of my life;
and I will dwell in the house of the LORD forever.

PSALM 23:5 NKJV

An Invitation

If you have ever:

  questioned if this is all there is to life...

  wondered what happens when you die...

  felt a longing for purpose or significance...

  wrestled with resurfacing anger...

  struggled to forgive someone...

  known there is a "higher power" but couldn't define it...

  sensed you have a role to play in the world...

  experienced success and still felt empty afterward...

then consider Jesus.

A great teacher from two millennia ago, Jesus of
Nazareth, the Son of God, freely chose to show our
Maker's everlasting love for us by offering to take all of
our flaws, darkness, death, and mistakes into His very
body (1 Peter 2:24). The result was His death on a cross.
But the story doesn't end there. God raised Him
from the dead and invites us to believe this truth
in our hearts and follow Jesus into eternal life.

*If you confess with your mouth that Jesus is Lord and
believe in your heart that God raised him from the dead,
you will be saved. –ROMANS 10:9 NLT*